Start-up Survival
for *first time* entrepreneurs

tried, tested and proven step to help you succeed

Uday Simha Prakash

Copyright © 2021 Uday Simha Prakash

All rights reserved.

ISBN: 9798504830735

DEDICATION

Vanessa, Maxmilian, Izabella.

CONTENTS

1. WHY I WROTE THIS BOOK 1
2. AUDIENCE 3
3. IDEA 5
4. TEST THE IDEA BY TALKING TO YOUR CUSTOMERS 7
5. MINIMUM VIABLE PRODUCT 9
6. WHY DOES ONE NEED TO DEVELOP AN MVP? 10
7. DIVING INTO THE REAL WORLD 13
8. FOUNDERS AND CO-FOUNDERS 15
9. CO-FOUNDER AGREEMENT 17
10. WHAT DOES A CO-FOUNDER AGREEMENT COVER? .19
11. REGISTERING YOUR COMPANY 21
12. TELLING THE WORLD ABOUT YOUR PRODUCT 22
13. MARKETING YOUR COMPANY 23
14. MARKETING CHANNELS 25
15. WEBSITE 28
    Hotjar 28
    Google Search Console 29
16. START YOUR MARKETING 30
    Google Ads 32
    Google Local Business 32
    Measure what Matters 32
    Google Analytics 33
17. BUILDING YOUR TEAM 36
18. PRICING YOUR PRODUCT 38
    Restaurants 39

    Subscription Software (SaaS) 39

    Delivery Service 40

    Break-Even Point 41

19. SELLING YOUR PRODUCT 45

    Prospecting 46

    Converting 47

    Closing 48

    Sales team 49

    Measure Performance 51

    Sales Representative Compensation 51

20. ACCELERATORS AND INCUBATORS 53

21. PITCH DECKS AND PITCHING 55

    Elevator Pitch 56

        15-second elevator pitch 58

        30-second elevator pitch 58

        60-second elevator pitch 58

    Pitch Deck 58

    Tips 62

    Tools to create your Pitch Deck 63

22. MENTORS 64

23. GENERAL GYAN 66

    "Faster - Better - Cheaper" 66

    "Be bad at something to be great at customer needs." 67

    "Zero cost marketing will save your butt as a start-up." 67

    "Get Close to Customers" 67

    "A story gets attention like nothing else." 68

24. TOOLS 69

ACKNOWLEDGMENTS

Experience, Failure, Perseverance and Grit.

Start-up Survival

1. WHY I WROTE THIS BOOK

In a letter to Robert Hooke in 1675, Sir Isaac Newton made his most famous statement: *"If I have seen further it is by standing on the shoulders of Giants"*. I echo the sentiments.

Have you ever felt like everyone else knows something[1], and they just are not telling you? No matter how close you get to the source of money and talent, you are just not about to cross that threshold?

I am writing this in my study in Bangalore, India, surrounded by entrepreneurs, both new and old, experienced and inexperienced, ones I know and do not. But just being in this entrepreneur rich environment puts me at an advantage over many others. Think about this in the year 2020, 9 now unicorns[2] were minted in India, according to Venture Intelligence[3]; out of these, 5 were in Bangalore. In 2021, up until May, there were already 13 new Unicorns, and 4 were from Bangalore. As of me writing this book of the 49 Unicorns in India, 20 are in Bangalore. This in itself makes Bangalore the Silicon Valley of India and draws immensely talented people here who are very happy to share their experience and nurture new and upcoming entrepreneurs.

---

[1] Straight Talk for Startups by Randy Komisar and Jantoon Geigersman
[2] Unicorn is a company that is valued at over 1 Billion US Dollars
[3] Venture Intelligence Unicorn Tracker – https://www.ventureintelligence.com/Indian-Unicorn-Tracker.php

What I have learnt is, it is not the big things; it is the little things—the wealth of broad experience, the tricks of the trade, wisdom shared by not only the winners but also the losers who have started and failed. Quoting the great Aerosmith[4] from their song Amazing, "life is a journey, not a destination," what is essential during the entrepreneurial journey is to learn from what didn't work and, most importantly, why it didn't?

To share what has been shared with me, this is why I wrote this book!

I have been inspired by a lot many authors, speakers, and fellow entrepreneurs. You will see their words echoed here[5] in the book. There is also a lot in this book from my own experience of having been at the helm of two start-ups.

There are many entrepreneurs who have helped me along the way. The best thing about being an entrepreneur is that your fellow entrepreneur is always there to help you – all you need to do is ask. I am hoping that this book will help someone in their journey.

---

[4] Aerosmith – Amazing https://www.youtube.com/watch?v=zSmOvYzSeaQ
[5] The original source is also quoted for you to refer to

2. AUDIENCE

This book is for those who have been toying with the idea of starting up. It is effortless for anyone to sprout an idea and believe that it is the next Unicorn. It all comes down to the execution of that idea you have; the difference between starting up and crashing and burning is execution. The legendary John Doerr[6] summed it up best when he said, *"We believe that ideas are easy, execution is everything, and in anything worth doing, it takes a team to win"*.

What I am trying to share is what I have learnt along the way, there have been many fellow entrepreneurs who have taught me things, so in a way, this is my homage to my fellow entrepreneurs who have skin in the game.

Many of you have been sold the idea that a start-up is; free food, unsupervised work, open layout offices, flat hierarchy, bean bags, and a lot of money at the end of the day. But being an entrepreneur is not just having fun but a lot of hard work, passion for your cause, immense meaningful innovation and at the end of the day, creating a business that adds value to the customers. This book is about how to make that idea you have a reality.

There are a gazillion books on shelves gathering dust, except a

---

[6] John Doerr: Best Entrepreneurs Attempt the Impossible ....
https://www.gsb.stanford.edu/insights/john-doerr-best-entrepreneurs-attempt-impossible

few which are excellent (I will be listing them at the end), that claim to teach entrepreneurship. The focus is on just the absolute essentials, the critical things, things that have been tried and tested. This book is in no way exhaustive because there is a lot to learn about entrepreneurship. What's touched upon is what is the absolute necessary points for start-ups younger than 2 years.

I have many people whom I need to thank, since that is not humanly possible, in no particular order I thank

A. N. Prakash, who let me play around with my ideas under his tutelage

Roshni Mohandas, my dear wife who put up with all my idiosyncrasies

Thomas K Joseph, who was is my mentor and an overall fantastic person to chill with

Beate, Devi, Surabhi, Khushboo, Krishnan, Vishal from my MPEFB batch

Professors P C Narayan, Shankar Venkatagiri at IIM-B

Nitthin, Nikhil, Chetan, Yogi, Abhi, Ama, Ashwin, Chetana from the SLP[7] 2019 Bangalore cohort

The team from Nemmadi.in and uniQin.ai who so tirelessly worked with me in spite of me.

---

[7] Startup Leadership Program – https://www.startupleadership.com/

We believe that ideas are easy, execution is everything, and in anything worth doing, it takes a team to win - John Doerr[8]

3. IDEA

OK, so you have an idea - so what? Many of them have an idea. What makes your idea different? Why should anyone other than you and your mother[9] believe that it is even worth its weight in salt?

As soon as we have an idea that we think and most certainly believe that it will amount to something, we tend to hide it from others. Wrong! If someone else wanted to do something similar, they would already have done so.

You have friends who know a bit about technology, the market, the way the local economy functions, professors in local colleges and most importantly, other entrepreneurs. What you need to do is talk to your circle of acquaintances - bounce the idea off of them, have a coffee or beer with them and tell them your idea. Ask them to tear holes in your idea and what you have thought of till now. This gives you two things - first, you get to see things from different points of view because (hopefully) not all your friends are cut from the same cloth. Second, if they poke holes in your idea, you get an opportunity to strengthen it by finding ways to address the problems they have so generously highlighted for you.

---

[8] https://www.gsb.stanford.edu/insights/john-doerr-best-entrepreneurs-attempt-impossible
[9] The Mom Test - Rob Fitzpatrick

This is not an easy process; you have just allowed people you know to get your idea that you know for sure (till then) will succeed. The initial instinct is to get defensive, don't. The moment you get defensive, your friends will sense it and stop giving you real constructive criticism. At this time, you need to be sure to listen over 70% of the time and make sure they talk. Ask them pointed questions like - "Why do you think my service that is like the Uber for Ambulances will not work in 2nd and 3rd tier cities like Mandya? After all, we have COVID amongst us". "Why do you believe that my growth of 200% month-on-month is too little?" You get the picture.

The secret sauce to this is to throw your idea to a variety of people because, at the end of the day, your service or product is likely to be used by a large spectrum of people. This way, you get their perspective early on, if not wholly, but at least a view that is not yours. Most importantly, you will have to speak to other entrepreneurs who have been on the journey one else or twice before. They will share with you experiential knowledge, not some random theory that can be read in any textbook.

When talking to them, don't be defensive; just either listen intently and absorb or if you are like me, take notes. After you have had your meetings, it is entirely your decision which of these nuggets of information you will use or not.

Towards the end of this journey, what you should have is a more concrete version of your initial idea. Now you would have been able to address many of the chinks in the armour, or at least you will be able to create a road map to manage them. In some cases, you may even decide that the initial idea was not worth it, and you nucleate a better idea. Essentially, it is imperative that you iterate over this process till you are satisfied and confident that you can go the mile and execute on this idea you have.

The best ideas originate when founders themselves are the users who are solving a problem they faced.

4 TEST THE IDEA BY TALKING TO YOUR CUSTOMERS

What you have till now is an idea, just a bunch of assumptions that you feel justify your time and others to hopefully one day generate money.

You already are way ahead of many of your peers; you are ahead because you have already spoken to your peers and have solidified your idea. It is now time to test it.

The primary thing that you need to get clear is your market, the people who want to pay for your product or service (henceforth, I will use "product" to refer to product or service, or them individually). You will have a general idea of whether people are willing to pay for it since you already have spoken to many about your idea (trust you have, if not, you better do it now).

It is time that you build a prototype of your product or offer your service to people. You and I know that you are still testing your idea, so the people who are gracious enough to try your early version of the service must know that it is not yet in its final version. This way, their expectations are set, and consequently, they will not bad mouth you if things fail.

In most if not the majority of the cases, entrepreneurs come up with ideas to solve problems they have faced themselves. This gives them an in-depth understanding of the problem, and they know that their solution will help solve it.

It does not matter if your closed set of testers agree to pay you for your service or not; you have someone from the real world who will put your idea through the wringer for you at practically no cost to you. My belief is if things are free, very few value them, so if you can convince them for a minimum of charge, even $1, then it's worth it.

What you want to be looking for when they are using your service is to see whether you are solving the problem they have?. Is it easy to use? Can you resell the service to them? Talk to them and listen intently; they will tell you what their expectations were and where you fulfilled them and where you were lacking. All your early testers will give you some insights into your service that are invaluable to you in terms of ease of use, perception of value add, the time they've taken to perform the task etc.

Remember that the perceived value that you bring to the table will help you set the price of your service.

You are now ready to make an MVP - minimum viable product.

The minimum viable product = *Only essential features with maximum value + maximum amount of validated learning with least efforts*[10]

5. MINIMUM VIABLE PRODUCT

Most failures result from poor execution, not unsuccessful innovation[11]

A minimum viable product (MVP) is a concept from Lean Start-up that stresses the impact of learning in new product development. Eric Ries defined an MVP as that version of a new product that allows a team to collect the maximum amount of validated learning about customers with the least effort[12]. As the name suggests, a minimum viable product should be something that you can send out into the world that has basic functionality, is reasonably reliable, fairly usable, and is not an eyesore in terms of design. That automatically means that you will fixate on that one value that you can bring to the product that a customer when they use the product will get a sense that there was value for money or more.

In any case, when you are at the MVP stage, you are either in closed beta or in beta, which means your customers know that the product is not fully functional and that it may not always work as expected - that is perfectly alright.

---

[10] https://www.spaceo.ca/minimum-viable-product/
[11] Straight talk for startups - Rule 5
[12] https://www.agilealliance.org/glossary/mvp/

6. WHY DOES ONE NEED TO DEVELOP AN MVP?

"This would never work in the real world." As entrepreneurs, we hear it all the time when you tell people about your great new idea. The best way to prove the nay-sayers wrong is to execute.

Fundamentally as a bootstrapped start-up, you don't have that kind of money to develop a full-blown product, and even if you did, you should not because you should definitely test the waters before diving in headfirst.

1. An MVP is an inexpensive proposition to enter the market and test the waters so that even in case of a failure, the problems, weakness, errors can be corrected in a short period and with not much expense. Some companies even use MVPs to test whether the proposition is an economically viable one or not. It all boils down to the fact that the concentration is on solving the customer's problem
2. Correctly done an MVP will give you great insights into your target group. The most important thing is to find out how willing people are to get out of their current comfort zone to try something new.
3. Once you know who the people are who are willing to use your product, you want to make sure that they actually want to use your product and the features that you so diligently

built. This will allow you to answer a few critical questions for better clarity on what your product should deliver for the customer to perceive value in it

- a. The problem you think you are solving is only in your mind, or does the customer actually encounter it?
- b. If it really is a problem, what are they currently doing to solve it? There are many who would just ignore it because it is not consequential or because the current solution to the problem is laborious. If it is the latter, you are in luck.
- c. If the customer does have a solution they are using and feel it is sufficient, you need to understand what inertia they have to overcome to jump to your solution. Essentially your solution should be an order of magnitude better, as explained in Peter Thiel's Zero to One - *"Anything less than an order of magnitude better will probably be perceived as a marginal improvement and will be hard to sell, especially in an already crowded market.*[13]"

4. Now that you have feedback from your client group use that to improve on your MVP by developing the suggestions made and rectifying the bugs. Now you are ready to go back to the people and show the app again, this time with improvements - this feedback loop will help you sharpen your product. This loop is important because when you share feedback with your customers, you build trust and establish relationships, finally allowing you to build brand loyalty.

5. Your presence in the market will mean that your competitors will know you exist, and in turn, you will know about them because your customers will tell you about them. Listen carefully you will learn a lot because the customers will tell you exactly what they don't like about the competition and why. Also, you will need to think laterally, just like airline companies realising that their completion today is not low-cost airlines, but the likes of Zoom, Skype, WhatsApp etc., who allow people to talk across the world without so much as leaving their room. It is not enough to think of just

---

[13] Chapter 3-5 of Zero to One – Peter Thiel | Genius. https://genius.com/Chapter-3-5-of-zero-to-one-peter-thiel-annotated

features, but you have to think of ways of solving the problems that the customer faces.

A few weeks of your feedback loop in place and your MVP development progresses with the idea that you are now able to talk to customers with confidence. Now you are ready to move into the real world and launch your product with a certain level of confidence because of all the work you have done to date.

When you are innovating and challenges come up that prove difficult and result in disappointment, although very difficult, it is good to not consider these as failures, especially since you have learnt from the approach and are able to refine your process.

If you are a non-technical founder, an MVP will help you temper the client expectations and give you absolute clarity on the deliverable. If you were to rely only on the word of your technical team and over-promise based on their assurances, you are most likely to compound your headaches. Yes, by moving methodically, your risk is you will not be able to scale quickly in the beginning if, for some unforeseen reason, the tech does not come together. Unless your competition is right behind you and breathing down your neck, this is the prudent way forward.

Remember, your company is better off with half of a great product rather than a full useless product.

The hard work starts now!

7. DIVING INTO THE REAL WORLD

Congratulations, you are now in the real world where people are not only going to pay you money for your service but also will burn you at the stake if you suck.

As I said earlier, this is where the real hard work starts - get ready!

There are many questions that a founder will have to face up to once they are at this stage (*in no specific order whatsoever*)
- Is it OK for me to be a solo founder? (If you are a set of co-founders, kudos to you)
- Do we, as co-founders, really need to get a co-founder agreement in place?
- What is a co-founder agreement
- Should I start hiring a team?
    - How large should the team be?
- When should the company website be launched?
- Should SMM[14] commence immediately?
- What channel of marketing is fit for us?
- Should we hire a salesperson immediately?
- What are incubators and accelerators?
    - How are they different?
- Do I get a Finance and HR person immediately?
- When does the funding journey start?

---

[14] Social Media Marketing

- How do we price our service?
- Why is positive unit economics important?
- Should we have ESOPs?
- What percentage of equity should I give my co-founders?
- What tools should we use to make our lives easier?

The list is almost endless... these are a few questions that are most frequently asked, and I will try to take you through the process where at the end, you should understand what your answer is.

Please realise that there is no one answer that fits all; this is very much like a bespoke suit. Each solution is specific to a start-up.

8. FOUNDERS AND CO-FOUNDERS

Most people whom I have spoken to and have interacted with are of the opinion that at least 2 founders of a company are a good idea. This even to this day remains a contentious issue; this paper by Greenberg and Mollick[15] argues that a solo founder is better.

There are many arguments for having a co-founder and not. What I have to say is this: if you are a single founder, don't go out looking for a co-founder. You will not find one quickly, and even if you do, there is no guarantee that it will work out. Finding a co-founder is more challenging than finding a spouse.

If you are a single founder, it's great you are the powerhouse behind the company, and it is your idea. There is nothing wrong with you being a single founder. Only in some instances does one need a co-founder. Such as, in case your idea needs technology and you are not a tech person, then you definitely need to find yourself a co-founder.

Be extremely cautious while doing so, don't be in a hurry. Take your time. You have to be absolutely sure you will get along and that you share the same vision. Take your time, better to be very safe than extremely sorry.

---

[15] https://papers.ssrn.com/sol3/papers.cfm?abstract_id=3107898

You are fortunate if when your idea germinated, you were not alone and have a co-founder by your side. It would be wise to, early on in the journey, clarify in writing what the role of each of the founders would be and what their responsibilities are. This would give all of you absolute clarity in your way forward.

As Albert Hold said and what is now widely generalised as Murphy's Law, *"when something can go wrong, it will"* that is the reason to get yourselves a "Co-Founder agreement".

9. CO-FOUNDER AGREEMENT

With all of the things that go into launching a start-up, it is rather tempting to avoid drafting your co-founders' agreement. The reason most of us argue with ourselves is, "We'll be good. We're all friends and co-workers. We absolutely trust each other. Most of all, we're in it together, having poured in money!"

And while all of that is very true, you definitely still need to get a co-founders agreement. Think of it as an insurance policy. One does not get insurance thinking one will get into an accident. It is there for when, unfortunately, one does. A co-founders agreement, like all other contracts, is there to help you not only navigate your day-to-day operations but also to comes to your aid when things don't go as earlier thought. It is a horrible idea to skip the co-founder agreement. Don't skip this step.

When you are starting a company, it's very easy to forget getting a co-founder agreement because there are many other burning issues at hand that need your immediate attention. This leads to you favouring your dreams and aspirations in place of technicalities.

When things are smooth sailing, there is no need for the agreement. It's not until you achieve some form of success and money starts to flow does do people have the propensity to change, and this is when greed comes into play. This is when many founders stop thinking about the vision of their companies and begin to think about themselves. For this very reason, it is imperative that all companies have a co-founder agreement in place signed and ratified.

10. WHAT DOES A CO-FOUNDER AGREEMENT COVER?

As co-founders, it is imperative that all of you sit together and discuss the various clauses in the co-founder agreement. This way, all the co-founders have buy-in, and all of you understand completely what each of your roles and responsibilities is.

Apart from the very obvious things that the agreement will have like the legal name of your company, the names of the co-founders, its address etc.,

In my opinion, a co-founder agreement should at the very least have the following

- Ownership Structure - This shows what percentage of the company each co-founder owns
- Initial Capital Contribution - How much each of the co-founders has/will contribute as founding members. The contribution may be in terms of money, time, assets, etc
- Tasks and roles - clearly list down what role each of the co-founders will be responsible for
- Expenses and Budgeting - up to what amount can a co-founder incur an expense on behalf of the company without the express written permission of the other co-founders.
- External Communication - who can and on what terms will

the co-founders communicate to the external world about the company, and only under what circumstances after approval by the co-founders
- Competition Restriction - any co-founder will not be allowed to work with any other company which directly or indirectly competes with the present company for a reasonable period of time after they part ways.
- Vesting and Reverse vesting of shares – this defines the time frame when the shares of the company will vest and also what happened if one of the founders decides to leave.
- Investment event – in case of external investment, what happens
- Buyback and disposal of shares – what are conditions under which the shareholders may sell their shared
- Intellectual Property – who owns the IP that is developed in the company
- Confidentiality – all founders will ensure that no inside information unless expressly permitted may be shared with the outside world
- Removal and departure of co-founders – under what circumstances may co-founders be removed
- Dispute resolution – the process to resolve an disputes

Apart from these, there are many other clauses that form part of the agreement. It is well-advised that you talk to a lawyer who has been around a few start-ups and knows what the current provisions in use are.

The easy way to find such a lawyer is to talk to a few incubators, accelerators and such. They have lawyers who work with them to make things easy for the companies at these places.

11. REGISTERING YOUR COMPANY

You or you and your buddies have started this fantastic journey from an idea to a product that you want to send out into the world in turn for money to do that and do that at scale. It is imperative that you have registered your own company—a legal entity that represents your idea and where all the assets and liabilities are.

In India, the first step is to make sure the name that you choose to represent your company is not already taken by someone else. Once that is out of the way, you and your co-founders will have to apply for a digital signature to sign the official documents with and also get your Director Identification Number or DIN.

A Company Secretary (CS) or a Chartered Accountant (CA) can do this for you. They will also help you generate your Memorandum of Association (MoA) and Articles of Association (AoA) for your company.

This is especially important if you are looking at funds from VC that are from outside of India. If they are American VCs, then they will, in all probability, insist on a Delaware Corp[16].

There is not much else for me to share here.

---

[16] Delaware corporations https://www.investopedia.com/terms/d/delaware-corporation

12. TELLING THE WORLD ABOUT YOUR PRODUCT

Congratulations, you are now on your way to becoming a Unicorn!

How does the world know that you exist? Why should the people you think are ideal for your product or service purchase your product or service? What makes you different from other fish in the sea?

You now have to cross these hurdles that are in your way and do so with aplomb.

How does the world look for what it needs? A search engine in all probability, and most likely than now they would use Google. So for you to stand a chance of being seen and heard in the noisy world, you need to stand out from the rest and list high up the Google search ranking.

Before all this, you definitely need to have a website. You do have a website, correct?

Get yourself a website today. If your product is not core to a website related subject, I will get a professional to do it so that you can concentrate on what your core is.

13. MARKETING YOUR COMPANY

What you definitely need to understand is that everything is marketing[17]. Let me explain what that means. The good folks in the marketing department are not the only ones who should be responsible for marketing your company. Marketing is something that everyone at your company should be responsible for all the time, except maybe for Finance and Accounting.

If you are not communicating about your company, the world doesn't know about you.

Remember that -
- Every time anyone within your company communicates with the outside world, be it via email, phone call, anything form of communication is marketing. Be it within the company or with the external world.
- The very experience that your customer has with your product is marketing
- Your website, with every single word and image on it, is marketing
- Remember your invoice can also be marketing when done properly

---

[17] Rework by Jason Fried and David Heinemeier Hanson

What you should recognise is that every touchpoint you have with your customer is marketing.

Allan Dib, who wrote "The 1-Page Marketing Plan," said it best. I quote him verbatim here.

*If the circus is coming to town and you paint a sign saying 'Circus Coming to the Showground Saturday', that's **advertising**.*

*If you put the sign on the back of an elephant and walk it into town, that's **promotion**.*

*If the elephant walks through the mayor's flower bed and the local newspaper writes a story about it, that's **publicity**.*

*And if you get the mayor to laugh about it, that's **public relations**.*

*If the town's citizens go to the circus, you show them the many entertainment booths, explain how much fun they'll have spending money at the booths, answer their questions and ultimately, they spend a lot at the circus, that's **sales**.*

*And if you planned the whole thing, that's **marketing**.*

14. MARKETING CHANNELS

You now understand what marketing is. But what channel suits your company? How much do you need to spend?

Before you go out and spend money on a newspaper ad or a TV ad, think about a few things so that you get the best RoI[18] for your marketing money.

Answering these questions will help you decide the channel most appropriate for you to spend your marketing budget on. Since most companies at an early stage are bootstrapped, it would be prudent on their part to spend any money very cautiously or have a zero cost marketing mentality.

1. At what juncture do the clients think about purchasing my product?
    a. Do they need to know the product exists a few months before the point of purchase, or can they make the purchase at any time?
    b. Based on your price point, will they take time to decide on the purchase?
    c. Is the purchase dependent on any external factor other than the customer's will? For example
        i. They need permission from somebody

---

[18] Return on Investment

        ii. They should have a completed a few other steps before your product is valuable
2. Are you a product that needs to be explained or is very easy to understand?
3. Are there others like you, or are you a relatively new product?
4. People will buy your product only once or multiple times
5. Is your product priced such that they can make the purchase online?
    a. Or do they need to see the product before the purchase?
    b. Or do they need to experience it
6. What is the demographic that your product will attract?

These will give you a better understanding of where you could advertise. Let me take you through an example of one company I am associated with and how we came to understand when and where we need to advertise.

At *Nemmadi,*[19] we know our service is appreciated by a client who is just about to move into his or her home. They would not be interested in our service if they are not in the market for a home, or they have only recently made a down payment for their home because the time for them to move into their apartment is relatively far away. Since our service (at the time of writing this book 2021) is a rather new service in India, they need to be explained as to what this service is and what it entails. The client comes to us only when the builder tells them that their apartment is ready to be checked, and then they can move into it. Once the client takes our service, there is no requirement for us at their home for the same service again. The way the service is priced, we know that people in India are not comfortable purchasing this service online but would instead transfer the money after having spoken to a company representative. And finally, we also know that the demographic we attract are the IT or ITES employees who are upwardly mobile and have travelled the world, so they understand what quality means.

Armed with all this information, we deduced the following
- Our customer will look for our service 1 to 3 months before they move into their new home

---

[19] https://www.nemmadi.in

- They will think about us only after their builder lets them know the date they can take over their new home
- Since they are paying in tens of thousands, they are comfortable if they see real faces in a video explaining what the service is and what value it brings them
- Clients will not pay for this service online

Now we get to what Marketing Channels these customers will most likely be available at
- Since it is all inbound marketing - Google Ads works well
- Since the demographic is mostly DINK[20] couples and the like - LinkedIn posts are ideal
- Because we need to explain the service with a human touch, YouTube videos are ideal
- As *Social Proof*[21] is a significant factor, we also used WhatsApp marketing with groups
- This then led us to *Referral Rewards*, where both the referring and the referred get a cash reward
- As most people like to read about what value they are getting for the money they plan to spend, technical articles on the Blog or Medium work very well

This way, you can narrow down the channels which work for you and which don't.

---

[20] Double Income No Kids
[21] https://en.wikipedia.org/wiki/Social_proof

15. WEBSITE

Maybe we got ahead of ourselves. We first need a functional and fast website that communicates what we do succinctly. Before we start our marketing campaigns.

All of us know that we definitely need a website. It need not be super complex. In fact, the simpler it is, the better. I will not be discussing the technical details of the website here. But what I want to discuss is how you can make sure that you are aware that your website is actually doing what it is supposed to and a few tools that you can use to ensure this[22]

Hotjar

I love this tool to understand where our clients click the most and what they are paying attention to.

---

[22] This is not an exhaustive list of tools

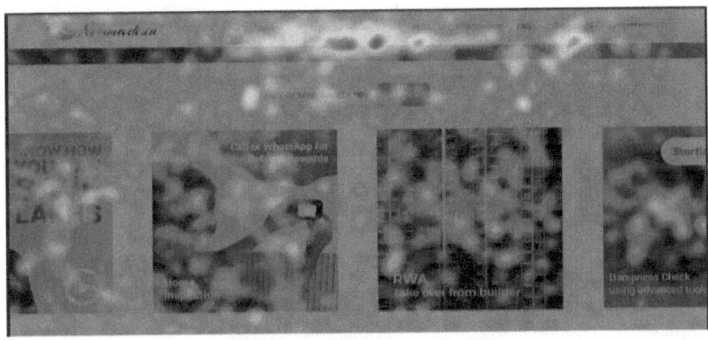

As you can see, the heat map shows that the design of the site is OK there are no dead spots.

You can also watch videos of customers interacting with your website.

this gives you information on how long they viewed the site, where did they interact with it, was it a mobile or a PC etc

Google Search Console
use it to check for links, external links and internal links. This may not give you the most in-depth information, but it gives you just enough for you to gauge the mood, so to speak

16. START YOUR MARKETING

If you have followed the steps, you are now ready to commence your SMM and marketing through channels other than online platforms.

I will be talking only about marketing using a specific few channels and not all. This is because these are what I am familiar with, and I know that they work.

Let us assume that your chosen channels for marketing are YouTube, LinkedIn, WhatsApp Business, Google Ads, WoM[23], BNI[24], Newsletters, Seminars.

To be able to publish on any and all of these channels, you will definitely be in need of the following
- Copy or content of the message
- Imagery

For the copy, use various keywords that convey your message succinctly. To generate the imagery, I personally use this fantastic tool Canva[25] that allows you to create images using stock images and various fonts. The greatest thing is there are templates for the

---

[23] Word of Mouth

[24] Business Network International

[25] https://www.canva.com/en_in/

different Social Media Channels you want to publish on.

Now that you have your content ready, your next step should be to publish on the various channels you've chosen. You can do this individually, which is time-consuming, or you can do it using one of many tools that are available, Hootsuite[26], Publer.io[27] etc. these tools allow you to not only publish the content across multiple channels at the same time but also help you schedule various posts into the future. This way you can set it and forget it for a week.

Video as a medium is an amazing place that you can generate a lot of value. Remember that YouTube is the second largest search engine after Google[28]. Your posts should not only optimise for Google but also YouTube. Create a YouTube channel that has your branding and contact details, all that is very easy to set up, and you should do it yourself. Once the basic setup is completed, you can start recording videos for your channel. There are a million videos on YouTube itself to show you how to do this, so I won't get into it.

But what I want to say is, it is a good idea to have real people, your company people, yourself as the founder and co-founders to be in the videos. This gives the videos a human touch and a face to your company. This way, you are closer to the people in the market for your product.

One unique channel that many people don't use effectively is the WhatsApp Business[29] app. Did you know you can register a landline number to your WhatsApp Business app? This way, you can receive messages on your mobile via WhatsApp directly from your website! Now all you need to do is create group links for specific customer groups and share them with people and get them to join the groups. This way, you have specific target groups on your WhatsApp to whom you can communicate with particular messages curated for them.

Google Ads is a powerful tool to use, and when used with some

---

[26] https://www.hootsuite.com/
[27] https://publer.io/
[28] The Best Content Marketing Formats [Research] - Heidi Cohen.
https://heidicohen.com/the-best-content-marketing-formats-for-your-business/
[29] https://www.whatsapp.com/business/?lang=en

research, it will bear bountiful fruit. I am not an expert on Google Ads. There are experts who can help you with this.

Google Ads

I trust you are not learning about this in this book — you definitely need to use it, primarily if your company provides a service or a product that is driven by pull marketing.

Google Local Business

Essentially use this to monitor your online reviews, how many photos you put in here and posts you make. This is a good place for your SEO. One can even set up a free site

These tools give you a handle on how your site content is being accessed and whether there is something missing or customers visiting your site are not able to understand. The next logical step is to enhance your SEO (which is a topic in itself and which we will not discuss in this book). Tools like Semrush[30], AHREFS[31], etc., will help you understand where you stand compared to your peers in your chosen subject. You can also use Google's own Keyword Planner Tool[32] to help you populate your website with the appropriate keywords.

Measure what Matters[33]

It's all good that you have started communicating with the world about what you do. Do you know the efficacy of your communication? Are you getting your money's worth? As Peter Drucker said, "*You can't manage what you can't measure*". I would add, "*you can't manage effectively what you don't measure*".

---

[30] https://www.semrush.com/
[31] https://ahrefs.com/
[32] https://ads.google.com/intl/en_in/home/tools/keyword-planner/
[33] A book by John Doerr

You are spending money online on Google Ads, and maybe even YouTube ads, Facebook Ads, Twitter Ads and in some cases, LinkedIn Ads. Offline you probably have printed some material to distribute, some brochures etc. Not only have you spent your money, but you have also spent your time; it is essential to know what this investment is getting you in return? Google Analytics is a great tool that helps you monitor various aspects of things on your website. Again there are many places where you can learn about Google Analytics; because of this, I will not go into that topic.

Google Analytics

This is a potent tool to have. Again I trust you already are using this in some capacity. You can improve the analysis by using Customisation. Kaushik's site[34] is a treasure trove of information too. Of course, you can also always take Google's course online.

Make sure you use customisation and the dashboard + custom reports.

Dashboards

CREATE
Name
Weekly SEO Troubleshooting Dashboard
Audience Overview
Content Analysis Dashboard
Goals and Channels Dashboard : Notify Dashboard
[GAT] Mobile Ecommerce Dashboard
[GOOGLE] : Site Performance Dashboard
[GOOGLE] : Social Media Dashboard
[GOOGLE] : AdWords Performance
SEO Dashboard
VP, Digital Dashboard

---

[34] https://www.kaushik.net/avinash/

There are many Custom reports one can choose from that suit your requirement. Some of the ones I use are in the image here. These will give you a chance to dissect the data and take decisions based on the data your website is providing you.

Start-up Survival

[Screenshot: Pageviews and Unique Pageviews by Page Title; Avg. Time on Page and Bounce Rate by Page Title; Exits and Pageviews by Page; Visits and % New Visits by Landing Page]

If you need fine-grained information, you can combine them.

[Screenshot: Users 8,455; New Users 8,371; Sessions 13,207; Number of Sessions per User 1.56; Pageviews 18,764. AK: Non-First, Potential L 830 / 668 / 1,102 / 1.33 / 5,258. AK: Loyal Visitors 472 / 0 / 2,425 / 5.14 / 3,840. [OAT] Really Engaged Tra... 280 / 202 / 378 / 1.35 / 2,679]

"Alone we can do so little; together we can do so much." – Helen Keller

17. BUILDING YOUR TEAM

Until now, you and your co-founder(s) worked tirelessly. You have been able to develop your MVP, your SMM is in full swing, your website is up and running. Now that you have started garnering interest in the community of potential customers, you will need to start on the working feverishly feedback loop development and problem handling. This means you have to expand your team.

Building your founding team is like laying the foundation for a multistorey building. It needs to be sufficiently deep and wide to bear the weight of the many floors that will eventually rise above. You will also have to keep in mind that you and your co-founders will be laying down the template for the culture of the company for many years to come.

Never compromise on talent. It is almost never a good idea to hire the second-best. As the old adage goes, "birds of a feather flock together." If your founding team is built with talent who are inquisitive, hard-working, and most of all ethical, the people who follow will be cut from the same cloth. For some reason, your hire is not the best you have met then; the hires that follow will also be second best or maybe even less desirable.

"To err is human.[35]" There will be instances that we do hire people who are not what they seem, or we may have been carried

---

[35] To err is human - https://en.wiktionary.org/wiki/errare_humanum_est#Latin

away by their words and not have delved into their actions. This is perfectly OK, now that you know that there is a misfit, act swiftly and replace the talent. A rotten apple can spoil the lot.

There may be many reasons for the talent not fitting in. It may just be a case of you trying to measure how far high a fish can climb a tree. Meaning, there are people who may have experience vast experience building a $100 million dollar company into a $500 million dollar company. Unfortunately, that is not the kind of experience you need while growing from a $1000 dollar company to a $5million dollar company. The skill sets are entirely different, the tools and levers that are used are completely different.

When speaking to people you want to join, ensure they are a correct fit for your company. Just because they have worked in a great company earlier doesn't mean they are a fit for yours.

It is essential that you have an open conversation with them and clarify for them what your expectations are, what role they will play and why the predecessor was let go or why you are creating the position at this juncture. Being transparent from the get-go is the best. This will avoid waste of time, money, and things are more straightforward for everyone involved.

As a fledgeling company measuring performance is not all that easy. This is because, in most if not all start-ups, most people fill multiple roles. As long as you and your co-founders are cognizant of this fact and acknowledge this transparently with your team, things will be good.

You have already chosen people who are up there in Maslow's hierarchy of needs[36] fulfilment. They have agreed to be part of your entrepreneurial journey because they want to fulfil their potential. It is also necessary for you to once in a while praise them and do so publicly.

In most cases, it is prudent to always push hiring new talent as far down the road as you possibly can. Unless, of course, you have signed contracts and need to fulfil them in the immediate future.

---

[36] **Maslow's hierarchy of needs -**
https://en.wikipedia.org/wiki/Maslow's_hierarchy_of_needs

18. PRICING YOUR PRODUCT

Your product is ready to be sold, but what is the correct price for your product? How do you price your product? What are the hurdles you face when pricing? Is my product priced too low? Is my product priced too high?

There are answers to all these questions, just that the answers vary depending on your product. We will take the journey of discovery together so that you can understand the process and some tricks of the trade.

First, you need to make sure every product you sell has positive unit economics. Unit economics for a specific business model refers to the revenues and costs in relation to an individual unit. A unit essentially refers to any fundamental, quantifiable item that is being sold that creates value for your business. That means positive unit economics demonstrates that with each item—or "unit"— you generate a profit for the company.

This essentially means that for every unit of sale, you make money for the company. For you to be able to calculate this, you would need to know the input costs of the product. Most discussions of unit economics focus on a specific metric called the *contribution margin*[37].

---

[37] Unit Economics: What is a Contribution Margin? - Outlier .... https://outlier.ai/data-driven-daily/unit-economics-contribution-margin/

Wait, what in the world is a 'unit'?[38]

Let's see what unit economics, aka contribution margin, is for a few different types of businesses.

Restaurants[39]

Each meal you serve is a unit, so the costs include the food you purchase and the time it takes to prepare the meal. The revenue is how much you charge for the meal, so your per-unit contribution margin is the

price you charge for your meal - (cost of the food + employee cost for making that meal)

You should not include the cost of the location or the cost of your furniture etc., as those are fixed costs that stay the same regardless of the number of meals you serve.

Subscription Software (SaaS)

Each subscriber is a unit, so the costs include how much you spend to acquire a customer, also known as CAC (Customer Acquisition Cost) and how much it costs to provide the service to them. The revenue for a customer is their Lifetime Value (LTV), which you can either estimate or calculate depending on your customer tenure. So your per customer contribution margin is the
LTV - CAC

You should not include your fixed costs, such as the costs of your servers, unless you need to add new servers for every customer. Similarly, assuming each customer uses the same software, you would not include the cost of developing the software.

---

[38] Every Unit Counts: Assessing Profitability | by Outlier AI https://outlierai.medium.com/every-unit-counts-assessing-profitability-90e0548dcc3e
[39] Unit Economics: Examples of Unit Economics - Outlier AI, Inc.. https://outlier.ai/data-driven-daily/unit-economics-examples-of-unit-economics/

Delivery Service

Each delivery is a unit, so the cost is primarily the payment you make to the courier who makes the delivery. More complex is the revenue you earn from a given delivery, which may either be a separate fee or an increase in the value of the product being delivered or a revenue share from the kitchen where the food is being prepared. So your per delivery contribution margin is the

Delivery Price - Cost of Delivery

As you can see, the challenge lies in separating your fixed costs from your variable costs and mapping those to your individual unit of business.

Contribution margin is a measure of your per-unit profit by subtracting the variable cost per unit from the sale price of the product. It is very similar to the Net Margin but is calculated at the individual sale level, which makes it more challenging to determine. For example, if you sell a product for $25 each and it costs you $10 to make each unit of product, your contribution margin per product is $15 or 60%.

The benefit of tracking your contribution margin is that you can easily do a break-even analysis, which shows how many units you need to sell to break even on your costs. For example, if your annual fixed costs (office space, administration, etc.) are $100k and the contribution margin for each item you sell is $5, you break even when you sell 20,000 units a year.

There is an excellent template[40] for the calculation of your BEP[41] on YouTube.

---

[40] https://www.youtube.com/watch?v=7MxlVMzRxa8
[41] Break Even Point

Break-Even Point[42]

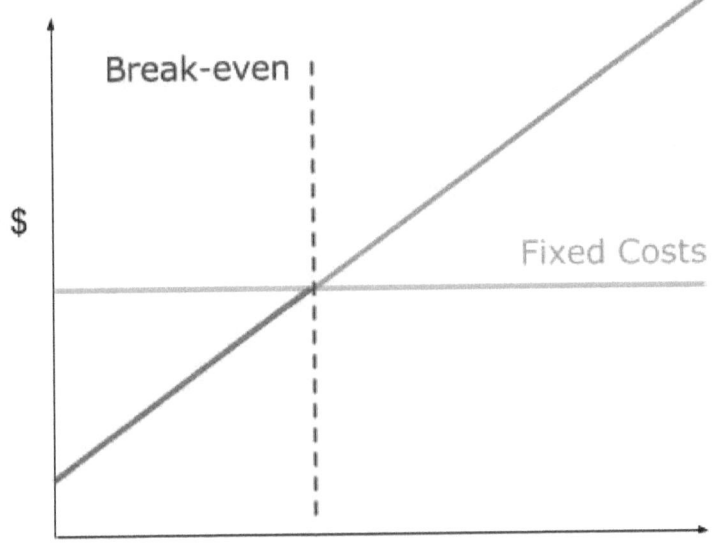

As you can see, as the number of units sold increases, the net revenue increases until it passes the Fixed Costs line, which is the break-even point. As long as the business sells more units than the Breakeven point, it will be profitable.

Now, in the real world, things are never so simple. Specifically, two factors will complicate your break-even analysis:

- It's likely that your fixed costs will go up with higher unit volumes. You might need more salespeople, more warehouse space or more manufacturing capacity. This means that your Fixed Costs can be a moving target, depending on volume.
- Economies of scale mean that your Contribution Margin may change as your unit volumes increase. Specifically, your COGS[43] should decrease over time because it will be cheaper

---

[42] https://outlier.ai/data-driven-daily/money-metrics-breaking-even/

to manufacture larger quantities of your product!

The result is a Break-Even analysis that looks more like the following:

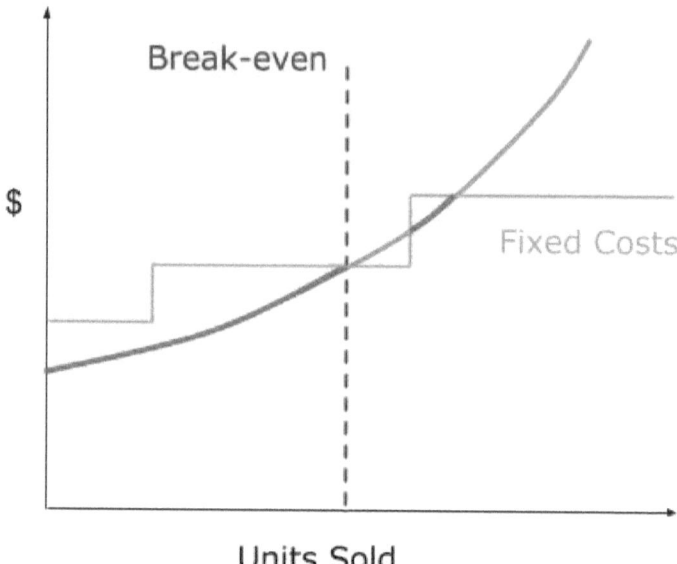

Note that there is not just one Break-Even point. There are two! That is because, in this example, there is a big jump in the fixed costs at a particular volume that exceed the growth in Contribution Margins. Such traps are critical to catching it before they happen, as you will be burning through capital when it does.

Now you are cognisant of the number of units you need to sell at your cost price with the contribution margin you have computed. Armed with this information, you, based on your type of product, have to decide whether you are now looking at selling elephants or bees[44]. Let me explain what this means. In the article, they are explicitly talking about SaaS[45] companies. This thought process does not apply only to SaaS products, though.

---

[43] Cost Of Goods Sold - https://www.investopedia.com/terms/c/cogs.asp
[44] http://christophjanz.blogspot.com/2014/10/five-ways-to-build-100-million-business.html
[45] Software As A Service

What Christoph is talking about is the effort is inversely proportional to the number of units to be sold. Let's assume that you want to sell your product for $10 (which I believe is over your cost price and has enough margins). You have also calculated the BEP in units that you need to sell to make a profit. It's evident that selling hundreds or even thousands of a product priced at $10 is relatively easy. Now think if your product is to be sold at $10,000 and you need to sell only 4 to make a profit. Obviously, you would take a lot longer to convince someone to make a $10,000 purchase than a $10 one, unless your product is very valuable in terms of making someone's life an order of magnitude easier or a desirable luxury item.

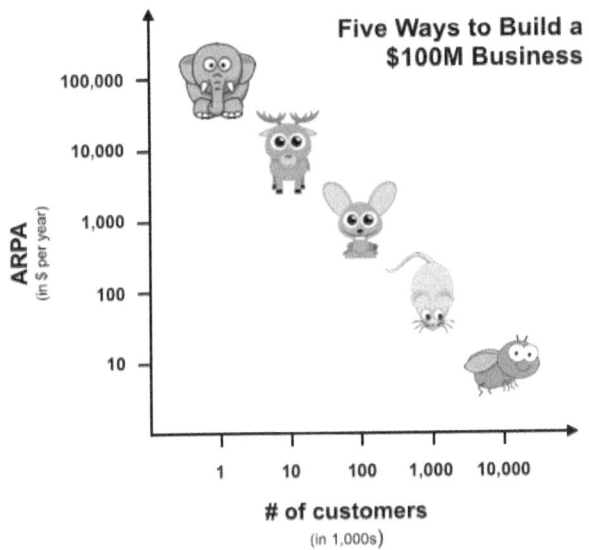

Now you know the effort involved in selling your product to your customers. This should give you a fair idea of the time and money you will need or what is generally referred to as *what your burn rate is*[46]? or *how much of a runway you have*[47]?

This is an easy and quick way to understand your pricing. There is a lot more here. You have your overheads, taxes, depreciation, amortisation etc., to make a beginning and to start selling without

---

[46] https://www.investopedia.com/terms/b/burnrate.asp
[47] https://www.brex.com/blog/startup-runway/

making a loss. These are what you will need to understand and execute.

19. SELLING YOUR PRODUCT

As a founder, what we all look for is predictable, scalable revenue growth. They are just four words, but they are powerful and also very difficult to achieve.

Before you go and hire a salesperson, it is imperative that for the first 100 customers, one of the founders performs this task. Unless you, the founder, performs the sales and understands the nuances of what it takes to convert a sale, you will not be in the right place. Let me explain. As a founder, you are passionate, you are still iterating over the product, and you are the only one who knows what your product does and how it enriches the lives of your customers. Now when you are out in the field and speak to customers, you will hear a lot of things that may need immediate action or some of them that are good to keep in your vault for action at a later point in time. This feedback from the customer to the engineering team helps bring to life what most customers want and need.

Paul Graham says this a lot *"as founders, there are two things you should be doing, at any point in time when you are starting your company, they are — talking to your users, and building your product"*. That "talking to your users" is the sales part! For many first-time founders, selling is very intimidating because many would never have made sales before. As I mentioned earlier, you, as a founder, is in a unique position that makes it possible for you to excel at sales. The first is the passion that made you a founder, and the second is the domain knowledge in line with the problem you are solving. You should realise that these two factors any day are a huge advantage over any sales experience anyone may have.

In sales, as everyone knows, there is the ubiquitous funnel with the various stages, viz prospecting, conversion, closing, revenue. What I will do is share with you a few strategies that not only we've used but also I've learnt along the way so that these four stages are not some nebulous concepts.

Prospecting

This is figuring out who will be interested enough to either answer your call or respond to your email or read your WhatsApp messages. For you to truly understand this, you will need to look at the technology adoption curve proposed by Everett Rogers

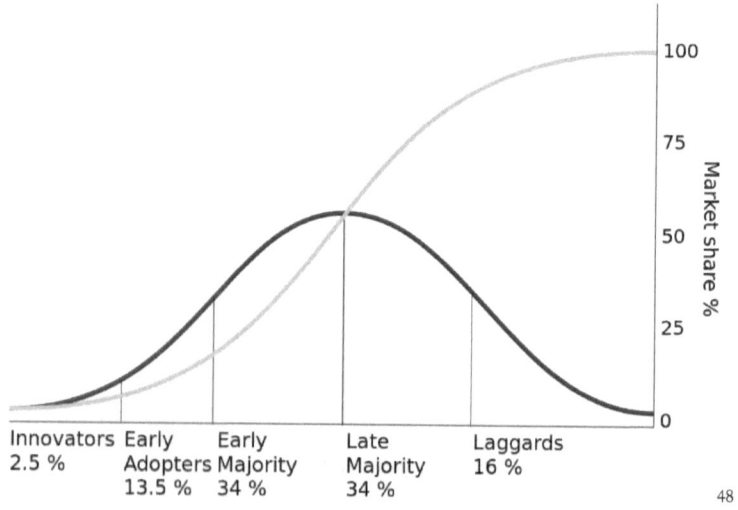

Innovators	Early	Early	Late	Laggards
2.5 %	Adopters	Majority	Majority	16 %
	13.5 %	34 %	34 %	

[48]

From this, it should be evident that your customers will be the innovators or the 2.5% of all people out there who are willing to try your product even though you are a start-up with no track record. This should immediately make it evident to you that all this comes down to is a number game. You will need to reach out to over 100 people to get potentially 3 customers. So where are you going to find

---

[48] https://en.wikipedia.org/wiki/Diffusion_of_innovations

these people? You can either curate them via the WhatsApp groups we spoke of earlier, your immediate network of friends. There are also formal business groups like BNI where you can meet with many potential customers. Cold emails are also a great way to reach out to people. Cold emails need to be succinct and to the point. Create a template that you can reuse multiple times this way, you save time.

Converting

The most important thing to remember is somewhat counterintuitive. Most of us would have the impulse to share what features your product has and go on to explain the value etc., but surprisingly the best thing to do is to listen to your customer, this is what the top salespeople — the top 1% of them in the world do — they listen 70% of the time. Most importantly, remember to ask a lot of questions that 30% of the time so that you learn more about your customer. Ask questions like — Why did they decide to talk to you? How do they solve the problem as of today? This way, you can understand the problem the customer is facing in-depth. This is what great sales is.

The other part of this stage is tireless follow-up. There are many numbers floating that talk about how many touchpoints before a sale etc., all that you need to know is customers have their own world that they live in, and their priorities are not aligned with yours. This means you will need to continually stay in touch with them to close your sale. You should be very thick-skinned to follow up, and it could be unnerving at times. A caveat to this is, as a start-up, you have minimal time, and this means you can't be on the phone forever. This means your goal should be to get the person on the phone to a yes or a no as soon as possible. Remember that it is always better to have a 'no' rather than a 'maybe'. The killer is if you have a massive set of "maybe's" because of this pipe dream, you will end up spending time unnecessarily. A 'no' is better than a maybe in many ways because that allows you to concentrate on the 'yes'. This means make sure you have a laser-like focus on your potential clients and, more importantly, on the correct pieces of the puzzle.

Closing

Woohoo! Now that your client has agreed to become a paying client, what comes next is your contract. In most cases, it is a good thing to share your agreement via a shared Google doc. This is useful to both you and the client because you can have both red-line the agreement. What red-lining means is the client can score out what they don't like, and you can also score clauses that your company doesn't agree on.

These templates for contracts are available at the YC library[49] if you don't have a contract as yet.

Please remember that your final goal is to sign a client. This means that it does not pay to haggle or to quibble over minor points or over a few clauses on your contract that does not have a direct bearing that is detrimental to your company.

The other trap that many founders fall for is believing clients who tell you that they will use your product if you were to build in one more feature. To most of us founders, when we hear this, we think, "Oh awesome, we can build this new feature, and they will use our product". But more often than not, it never works that way because more often than not, if you build the feature and go back to them, there will be just one more feature for you to build for them. The ways that you can go about if this happens is to politely pass on them as a client, which is very hard to do but the best thing. Build the feature if many other clients also ask for it and then go back to them with the feature built. Or sign a contingency contract with them.

One of the biggest traps that you definitely have to avoid is the 'free trial' trap. You may be thinking, but why? I am getting a customer. But are you? As a start-up, early on, you need — commitment, validation and revenue. A free trial gets you none of these. The way around this would be to offer them an annual contract which allows them a free no-questions-asked 30 day cancellation period with full money back for the unused period on the contract.

---

[49] https://www.ycombinator.com/library

The chart that Christoph developed and shown earlier is also helpful here to understand how your Sales team will be formed. For the products represented by Elephants, you will need to field a sales teams. For those by Deer, you will be able to manage with inside sales teams. For the remaining, marketing would suffice.

Sales team

Mark Roberge[50] , a Harvard Business School professor, starts his talk by asking-- "*What is the failure rate of a Series A start-up if you measure failure as they don't even give back money to the investors? What about Series C start-up? You are further along*" The surprising answer to this is 75% for both!

Continuing his thought process, think about this -- plot a graph with the x-axis with two quadrants mediocre revenue growth and awesome revenue growth, y-axis with two quadrants mediocre revenue retention and awesome revenue retention. Which path, according to you, is the optimal path for growth. The ideal quadrant to be in obviously is quadrant 4, but what is the optimal path to reach there? Many would say it's best to increase revenue to awesome levels and then increase your revenue retention and finally reach quadrant 4. Counter Intuitively, what's actually good for you is to achieve high to awesome revenue retention and then be able to throttle your growth. Think about it. It is because you now have fuel to feed your growth machine.

With this paradigm in mind, if you think about what revenue really is, you will realise that revenue is actually an outcome of value creation. This is very evident with the online behaviour of people when they are researching products. The first thing they do is to go online and search for reviews about the product. A product that brings value to its customer will naturally have a lot of positive reviews. When does a customer leave a positive review? It is most likely to be when they have an "aha moment", in other words, when they feel a level of satisfaction they expected, or you exceeded their expectations. Some examples that Mark shares of products and their "aha moment."

[50] https://www.youtube.com/watch?v=alAbNeqn9K8

- Slack -- a team sends over 2000 messages between themselves
- Dropbox -- a user added a file to a folder on a connected device
- Hubspot -- someone using 25% of the features within 60 days of registering

This 'aha moment' is a leading indicator that you need to be aware of your product usage and monitor it religiously to see that you improve on it.

% of customers that achieve leading indicator status by month of tenure

Customers Acquired	Month	1	2	3	4	5	6	7	8	9	10	11	12
24	January	3%	27%	33%	37%	40%	39%	44%	45%	45%	52%	55%	56%
26	February	2%	26%	30%	36%	38%	40%	38%	42%	43%	44%	49%	
29	March	3%	27%	34%	40%	43%	46%	49%	50%	49%	53%		
38	April	5%	43%	58%	64%	68%	68%	71%	73%	70%			
43	May	4%	49%	58%	63%	66%	71%	69%	73%				
41	June	3%	39%	48%	59%	65%	71%	73%					
37	July	5%	40%	50%	62%	70%	72%						
39	August	7%	56%	72%	76%	81%							
50	September	12%	68%	75%	77%								
55	October	6%	70%	78%									
48	November	9%	73%										
49	December	9%											

The graph shows in January only 27% of customers reached the aha moment in month two, whereas in October that number had risen to 70%. This is when you have product-market fit, as you are creating value for the customer.

This is the basis for your sales team hires. Of course, the founders will be making the sales for the first 100 customers. Then after that, using these leading indicators, you should hire new sales representatives. For the next few hundreds of customers, you will need to hire a sales guy who is a mix of a product manager and a seller. This means this person will have the capacity to get back to the engineering team and communicate in a cogent manner that something is not in sync with what is being developed and what the customers need. This continuous feedback loop will help in improving your product-market fit and go-to-market.

Most importantly, you as the founder have to make sure the Sales and Marketing teams are aligned. Both the teams have to talk and understand which channel generates better revenue and how Marketing can generate leads from them for Sales to close.

Measure Performance

It is almost impossible to measure the performance of a marketing person or an engineer, but a sales rep's performance can easily be measured.

The way to do it is to set up a company-wide Sales SLA. These are measured every day, and the dashboard regularly shared with the sales teams. This makes sure all of them know where they stand. What are these SLAs?

Depending on your company and the product you're selling, you can have something like this --
- All new incoming leads need to be contacted within one hour
- Stay in touch with established leads who are not communicative at least 4 times in 7 days
- Continue to stay in touch with them at least 10 times in 30 days
- Close the sale within 60 days
- Archive the contact if dragging over 90 days

This will help you see which of your sales team members are performing and who is not.

Sales Representative Compensation

It is common knowledge that sales reps jump ship every 2 or 3 years, but why is that? Why are they not staying even though you have trained them and compensated them so handsomely? Or have you?

I believe that you can retain these guys and make sure they perform well by linking their compensation with the revenue. Here is what works for a few of us. An entry-level Sales Associate can have 75% fixed, 25% variable and a performance-linked incentive (PLI).

Similarly, a Sales Manager could have 65%, 35% and PLI etc. The important part is to set their goals keeping them in confidence right off the bat. You should also look at sharing with them a threshold that they have to cross to get a promotion.

This makes the process completely transparent and incentivises the sales team to perform, and most importantly, they will stick with you for longer.

20. ACCELERATORS AND INCUBATORS

Oftentimes entrepreneurs entering the start-up arena are exposed to the business vernacular. Unless you are one of these brave souls, who is peddling your brilliant new idea, have a background in commerce, you will find yourself lost in conversations with people throwing around terms like an angel investor, crowdfunding, seed funding, VC (venture capital), PE (Private Equity), Incubator, Accelerator -- this list continues to grow daily. One of the biggest and fundamental misconceptions early entrepreneurs have is that accelerators and incubators can be used interchangeably, which could be forgiven but sadly incorrect.

There are many great articles on the differences and uses etc. But the only way to know the efficacy of one is to participate. Before you dive in, make sure you are getting your time's worth because you can make money again but will never get back your time. Before selecting a program, talk to a few people who have been through the program, ask them pointed questions based on what you want out of the program so that you can make a calculated decision.

At the end of the day, it is entirely up to you to get the most out of the program. The more you dig, the more you get. I, for example, made a fantastic network of friends who are also entrepreneurs. This means they are a phone call away in case I need any guidance or help. Not only are my immediate cohort available, but also the whole fraternity that has been through the program. Most programs have a demo day, where you get to pitch your idea to a set of invited investors who, if they like what you have presented, may decide to immediately invest in your start-up.

Accelerator	Incubator
Expedite growth with an MVP	Develop your business idea
Set time frame to receive mentorship and networking	Most operate on a flexible time frame ending
Have a formal entrance selection process and a lot more exclusive	Invest time and resources to develop and nurture local entrepreneurs
Both provide mentorship and networking	
Do invest a specific amount in companies in exchange for a predetermined percentage of equity	Do not traditionally provide start-up capital or take an equity stake in companies

That conveniently brings us to pitching and pitch-decks.

21. PITCH DECKS AND PITCHING[51]

Starting a company is a laborious process. Getting outside funding is many times a necessary step for many start-ups. Fundraising is an opaque and convoluted process, especially for those who are at it for the first time. Pitching and pitch decks are an integral part of this journey.

We know coming up with creative ideas is easy; selling them to strangers is very hard. This is where execution comes into the picture. All too often, we entrepreneurs go to great lengths to show how our new business idea is practical and has high margins—only to be rejected by powers that may be, who don't seem to understand the actual value of the ideas. Why does this happen?

Research shows that the problem has as much to do with the seller's (entrepreneur) traits as with an idea's inherent quality. The person on the receiving end tends to gauge the pitcher's creativity as well as the proposal itself

We all like to think that people judge us carefully and objectively on our merits. But the truth is, they are in a hurry to pigeonhole us into little preconceived categories—essentially stereotype us. So the first thing you have to realise when you're preparing to make a pitch

---

[51] How to Pitch a Brilliant Idea - Harvard Business Review. https://hbr.org/2003/09/how-to-pitch-a-brilliant-idea

to strangers is that your audience is going to put you into a box of their liking. And they're going to do it really, really fast. Research suggests that humans can categorise others in less than 150 milliseconds. Within 30 minutes, they've made lasting judgments about your character.

When you are pitching your idea to a person you don't know, they search for visual and verbal cues and match those cues with their preconceived models, all the while remembering only the one or two characteristics of the pitcher, i.e., you to box them. They subconsciously award people they can quickly identify as having creative traits; and punish people who are hard to assess or who fit negative stereotypes.

Now imagine when you are pitching to a VC, it is a hurried business situation in which they must evaluate dozens of ideas in a week or even a day. These VCs are rarely willing to spend that extra energy necessary to judge an idea more objectively. Most likely, they will use negative stereotyping to rapidly identify flawed ideas. According to an article published in The Harvard Business Review[52], all you have to do is fall into one of four common negative stereotypes, and the pitch session will be over before it has begun.

In fact, many such sessions are strictly a process of elimination; only 1% of ideas make it beyond the initial pitch.

You essentially have between 30 and 60 seconds to convey your idea to a person judging you in the initial rounds, and if you succeed here, you have upwards of 3 to 10 minutes in rare cases.

Elevator Pitch

According to Wikipedia, this is the definition of an elevator pitch[53] — *"An elevator pitch, elevator speech, or elevator statement is a short description of an idea, product, or company that explains the concept in a way such that any listener can understand it in a short period of time. This description typically explains who the thing is for, what it does, why it is needed, and how it will get*

---

[52] https://hbr.org/2003/09/how-to-pitch-a-brilliant-idea
[53] Elevator pitch - Wikipedia. https://en.wikipedia.org/wiki/Elevator_pitch

done. Finally, when explaining an individual person, the description generally explains one's skills and goals and why they would be a productive and beneficial person to have on a team or within a company or project. An elevator pitch does not have to include all of these components, but it usually does at least explain what the idea, product, company, or person is and their value."

Yeah, I know it is rather a mouthful. What essentially is the need for an elevator pitch? By definition, it comes from the concept that you are riding an elevator and a person whose attention you want to grab enters, and they will get off in a few stops that means you essentially have 30 seconds to convey your message in a way that grabs their attention and they also, more importantly, remember what you have said.

Pitching is an essential tool in your arsenal in engaging with the audience. Today's audience is not only very fickle but also are continuously on their mobile with a very short attention span. This means that you have a very short time, few seconds in fact, of undivided attention. If you are unable to interest them in these few first seconds, they will tune out.

The essential ingredients of a good elevator pitch are

1. The primary object of the pitch is to grab their attention — Essentially, your elevator pitch is like a movie trailer or a blurb of a book on the dust jacket. You know you have mastered it when they ask you a question.
2. Make it all about them, and what they will gain — you build trust by making them the centre of the idea, this way, you build a great rapport.
3. Keep your focus on the main point — you have all but 30 or 60 seconds to convey your point, which is not sufficient time to talk about yourself or about many points. A good pneumonic to follow is KISS — Keep It Simple Stupid[54]. A great concept to follow is
    a. One central idea
    b. One hurdle you will help overcome
    c. One promise
4. Paint a mental picture — for them in their mind's eye to see how positively different their life will be for them.

---

[54] KISS principle - https://en.wikipedia.org/wiki/KISS_principle

5. Constantly practise your pitches and sharpen it with every time you make it to an audience, be it an audience of 1 more many

15-second elevator pitch

- Your name and what your role is
- The value you are bringing in 15-20 words
- How is their life-changing positively for using your product?

30-second elevator pitch

- Your 15-second elevator pitch plus
- Some data, quantification and a story

It is always great to have a story, for, e.g. "a cat sat on a mat", won't do very good, but if you were to say "the cat sat on the other cat's mat", then you automatically imagine things and form a mental image that will stick with you even after I am gone

60-second elevator pitch

- Your 30-second elevator pitch
- You also identify in a deeper manner the problems they face and show that you understand
- Elucidate what you do in a straightforward fashion

End with a call to action—a meeting or a call etc

Pitch Deck

While you are practising your elevator pitch, it's also vital that you develop your crisp pitch deck. DocSend[55], a start-up that specialises in providing an interesting way of sharing files with investors, studied over 200 pitch decks[56] to figure out the optimal set of slides in your

---

[55] https://www.docsend.com/
[56] https://docsend.com/view/p8jxsqr

pitch deck to graduate from a bootstrapped company to a funded company.

Lessons from a study about pitch decks by DocSend[57]

- VCs spend an average of 3 minutes 44 seconds on a deck
- An average of 40 investors was met
- Took around 12 weeks to close a round
- There is no correlation between more meetings and more funding
- Find VC firms who are aligned with what you are doing, target them first
- Counter-intuitively, seed rounds moved faster than an angel round
- 10 slides that are a must for a successful deck[58]
    - Company purpose — This is not much different from the so-called elevator pitch. Briefly say what you are doing and why. It is beneficial to start off by saying as clearly as you can what you are in terms that the audience is likely to understand. For example, "We deliver groceries to customers in their homes" is more explicit than "we are a next-generation, AI-based resolver of grocery needs." This is sometimes called a mission statement, but regardless, strive for conciseness and clarity. A common error is to avoid describing what you do until far into the presentation. That is always a mistake.
    - The problem you are addressing — In almost every case, a simple description of the problem your product solves should be a part of your presentation. However, beware of the caveat above, and do not spend too much time describing your

---

[57] Lessons From A Study of Perfect Pitch Decks: VCs Spend An ....
https://techcrunch.com/2015/06/08/lessons-from-a-study-of-perfect-pitch-decks-vcs-spend-an-average-of-3-minutes-44-seconds-on-them/
[58] A Guide to YC Demo Day Presentations: Fundraising, Pitch ....
https://www.ycombinator.com/library/49-a-guide-to-yc-demo-day-presentations

problem leading up to your fantastic solution and leaving the listener wondering what, exactly, you do until half your pitch is done.
- Your unique solution — Explain in more detail what you are building and for whom. This used to be where you would show a demo, but ironically, demos seldom work in modern demo day presentations. Explaining rapidly and clearly what your product does can be the most challenging and rewarding part of getting ready for a demo day.
- Why now is the correct time — Why do you, as the founder, expressly feel that right now is the perfect time for your idea to flourish? The confluence of what makes the atmosphere the most conducive?
- What is the Market size you can address — This is usually expressed as a total addressable market (TAM). It is vastly better to be concrete and bottoms up (e.g., "We can sell for $X, and we have Y potential customers, leading to an addressable market of $X * Y") rather than nebulous and top-down (e.g., "The software market is a $15 trillion dollar market…and if we can capture just 1% of that market…"). Your goal is to persuade the audience that the opportunity is real, that you are not making up data out of thin air, and that your company has a real shot at the dollars you describe.
- Your product that provides the solution — What is it that makes your product different from the myriad other ones in the marketplace currently vying for the top position.
- The team — How you integrate your team into the presentation is up to you, but it is crucial to keep in mind that investors are investing in you and your team above all, and therefore to generate interest, you must sell the team. However, realistically you cannot do much during this brief presentation, so only spend time here on truly notable aspects of the team ("Jill has a PhD in rocket science and holds the patent on the core technology upon which this market is built.").
- Business model — investors believe you have one.

Sometimes the model is obvious, and it is unnecessary to belabour it ("we are a new kind of retail store"), but even in these cases, it may be necessary to explain why you will be profitable. Few in the audience will believe a model where unit economics seem impossible. You do not have time to elaborate and explain your model in detail. Therefore you must find a way to describe it in simple and easy to retain terms.

- o The competition — who, according to you, is the competition? Don't ever say there is no competition. That only will show you have not done your research thoroughly enough.
- o Financial projection — By demo day – thanks to the current era of shareware, frameworks and AWS – most companies are up and running, accepting customers, and, hopefully, growing like weeds. Here is where you get to show your weed-like growth. Bring out your hockey sticks and show us your start-up growth curves. Sure, you have a great story - but now is the chance to persuade listeners that it is non-fiction. What happens if you have no traction or have not launched? This is not the end of the world. Many start-ups have successfully presented their companies pre-traction, but you must keep in mind that in that case, your success rests on the power of your story to persuade. You will be forced to lean more heavily on your personality and credentials, your story, and on your dream.

- Which of these slides were paid the most attention to

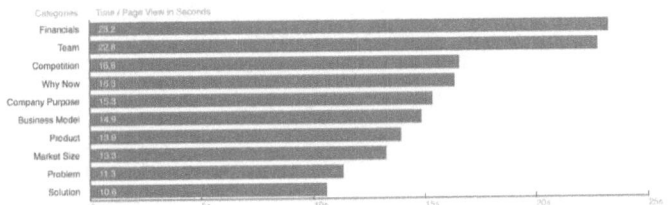

Tips

Creating great slides is an art form that great presenters learn to master. Keep in mind that your slides are your support, not your competition.

Keep the following tips in mind:

- A slide should have one central point, never more.
- Use pictures rather than words whenever possible, and make them relevant and additive to your point. In other words, the slide should be an aid to making your point clear. If it is neutral or confusing, it would be better if it weren't there.
- Minimise the number of words on a slide. If there are words, they should be in a very large font. If you have more than 7 words on a slide, it is likely to be too many.
- Quotes are great, but make them prominent and read them aloud to your audience to emphasise the point. Don't expect the audience to read a quote while you say something else.
- If you have images and text, make sure the text is in an area that provides contrast so it is readable. If necessary, add a semi-transparent background to the text.
- Make sure fonts are large and easily legible from a distance. Likewise, do not choose colours that wash out easily or are hard to see. Primary colours or black are usually safe choices.
- Put important text at the top of the slide. People sitting in the back of an auditorium may not be able to see the lower part of a screen.
- Avoid cumulative graphs. By definition, these always show growth - up and to the right - and always cause immediate suspicion that there is no real growth.

YC has a fantastic blog post on this very topic[59]

---

[59] https://www.ycombinator.com/library/49-a-guide-to-yc-demo-day-presentations

Tools to create your Pitch Deck

Your pitch deck needs to be crisp and have few words and more imagery. The idea behind this is that the attention of the audience is on you and the deck is only as an aid or a tool to let them know what you are speaking about.

One of the best presenters was SteveJobs. Take a look at his presentations. The slide has either an image and no words, and if there were any words, they were few and far between. The attention was always on Steve Jobs. This is how your deck should be.

There are many tools that allow you to create your pitch deck—Microsoft PowerPoint, Canva, Slidebean[60] etc. My favourite is Canva for its sheer flexibility and the myriad templates they have.

---

[60] https://slidebean.com/

22. MENTORS

Find yourself a mentor.

As a founder of a fast-growing start-up, you are on an extremely fast-paced and steep learning curve. The livelihoods of your employees and yourself, along with a lot of money, is at stake to not take this seriously. It is imperative that you don't fail. In fact, you can't afford to fail. When you were in school, you had a teacher who helped you with your learning. Similarly, in your entrepreneurial journey, you need someone who can help you surmount the hurdles, push you to your limits, push your buttons to ensure your company succeeds. Don't be surprised if your mentor decided that you would need to be replaced by a professional CEO. After all, this is for the good of the company. Faking it till you make it won't work here!

There are many terms bandied around for the role this person plays — adviser, coach, mentor. Realise they are not the same.

An adviser fills in the missing pieces in your puzzle. They bring in crucial missing expertise and experience. Their role is to advise you in areas that are outside of your strengths and experiential knowledge. Theirs is a very tactical role. Advisers essentially help you become a more knowledgeable CEO

A coach, like a sports team coach, is there to improve your skills. Their primary objective is to make you fit for your job. They will help you with things you are lagging in, leadership, communication style at that juncture. As a coach, they bring in a lot of insight and help you cross that immediate hurdle. Coaches make you a more skilled CEO

A mentor is like the rarest of gems — tanzanite, rarer than diamonds. They take you under their fold and improve you as a whole person. They are there to make you a better person overall, not just as a leader or as a CEO. A mentor will invest in you personally. They may not necessarily invest in your venture, though. At the end of the day, mentors make you a better you.

Finding a mentor is not an easy task. First, there are few and far between people who have the capacity to be a mentor and even fewer good mentors. Essentially the chemistry between you, the mentee and the mentor has to be remarkable. They should know you, know of you, and importantly they have to believe in your talent, character and passion. Another facet of a mentor is they will tell you the unadulterated and unvarnished truth, this will hurt, but it is necessary for your good.

As a founder, it is your duty to look for an adviser who can make you smarter. You could also look for a coach to improve your skills. And if you are one of the lucky few, you will get yourself a mentor to make you great.

One thing to remember is what the great mentor Bill Campbell was famously known to say —"*you can't coach height*", meaning that either you have it or you don't. This is why when you come up to your limits, a mentor will advise you to find a suitable replacement.

23. GENERAL GYAN

Here I share anecdotes from a few of the people with whom I have had the fortune of interacting. They are running multiple-million dollar companies, spanning multiple cities; many of them have been start-up founders many times over.

∎∎∎

"Faster - Better - Cheaper"
— Vaitheeswaran[61]

As the person who set up India's first online shopping site Indiaplaza.com, he shared a lot of his experience.

The essence of what he shared could be summed up into if you are in the field and can do something that is "faster, better and cheaper" than your competition, you will leave the competition in the dust. Most innovations will get you two of the three, but the holy grail is all three. Uber, Google and many more got all three right.

---

[61] https://in.linkedin.com/in/kvaitheeswaran

"Be bad at something to be great at customer needs."
— Srikanth Iyer[62]

A 4X founder-entrepreneur, he has vast experience that he gladly shared during many sessions face to face and over the phone.

The idea is you can't be the best at everything. This will make you the worst at everything. You know what your client needs and how you can bring value to them. Armed with this knowledge, decide what you will be relatively bad at so that you can be the best at many more important things that truly add value to your customers.

■■■

"Zero cost marketing will save your butt as a start-up."
— Ganesh Balakrishnan[63]

A 3X founder and a marketing genius. While sharing the various tools they build in their armoury to gain new customers, the gold nugget was to find these essentially Zero cost marketing tools that can help market your product, but you incur no cost. Let me elucidate, he spoke of how his team was able to incentivise waiters and servers in restaurants and bars to have patrons use their product because it helped these waiters and servers get tips. So it was in their interest to have customers use the app. Essentially the company selling the app incurred no cost at all.

■■■

"Get Close to Customers"
— Vaibhav Tewari[64]

Also, a 3X founder, his go-to phrase for a fledgeling start-up is

---

[62] https://www.linkedin.com/in/iyersrikanth
[63] https://www.linkedin.com/in/ganeshbalakrishnan
[64] https://www.linkedin.com/in/vaibhavtewari

GCTC. Make sure you are there right next to your customers. Always be there asking questions, providing after-sales services, and learning how to improve your current product. The customers are the only ones who truly matter and can tell you precisely what they need.

"A story gets attention like nothing else."

Imagine listening to "a cat sat on the mat", in your mind, you have no imagery that excites you. The whole idea of a cat sitting on the mat is absolutely mundane. Now, what comes to mind if you were to hear "a cat sat on the other cat's mat", immediately your mind conjures a catfight at the very least. This is because you listened to an exciting story. Similarly, when you are talking about your product, it is advisable to share it as a story that enables them to remember you.

24. TOOLS

List of tools[65]
List of books
List of useful URLs

---

[65] Start-up Survival Links - http://bit.ly/StartupSurvivalLinks

Footnotes

1. Straight Talk for Start-ups by Randy Komisar and Jantoon Geigersman
2. Unicorn is a company that is valued at over 1 Billion US Dollars
3. Venture Intelligence Unicorn Tracker – https://www.ventureintelligence.com/Indian-Unicorn-Tracker.php
4. Aerosmith – Amazing https://www.youtube.com/watch?v=zSmOvYzSeaQ
5. The original source is also quoted for you to refer to
6. John Doerr: Best Entrepreneurs Attempt the Impossible ....https://www.gsb.stanford.edu/insights/john-doerr-best-entrepreneurs-attempt-impossible
7. Startup Ledership Porgram – https://www.startupleadership.com/
8. https://www.gsb.stanford.edu/insights/john-doerr-best-entrepreneurs-attempt-impossible
9. The Mom Test - Rob Fitzpatrick
10. https://www.spaceo.ca/minimum-viable-product/
11. Straight talk for start-ups - Rule 5
12. https://www.agilealliance.org/glossary/mvp/
13. Chapter 3-5 of Zero to One – Peter Thiel | Genius. https://genius.com/Chapter-3-5-of-zero-to-one-peter-thiel-annotated
14. Social Media Marketing
15. Solo Survivors: Solo Ventures Versus Founding Teams https://papers.ssrn.com/sol3/papers.cfm?abstract_id=3107898
16. Delaware corporations https://www.investopedia.com/terms/d/delaware-corporation
17. Rework by Jason Fried and David Heinemeier Hanson
18. Return on Investment
19. https://www.nemmadi.in
20. Double Income No Kids
21. https://en.wikipedia.org/wiki/Social_proof
22. This is not an exhaustive list of tools
23. Word of Mouth

24	Business Network International
25	https://www.canva.com/en_in/
26	https://www.hootsuite.com/
27	https://publer.io/
28	The Best Content Marketing Formats [Research] - Heidi Cohen. https://heidicohen.com/the-best-content-marketing-formats-for-your-business/
29	https://www.whatsapp.com/business/?lang=en
30	https://www.semrush.com/
31	https://ahrefs.com/
32	https://ads.google.com/intl/en_in/home/tools/keyword-planner/
33	A book by John Doerr
34	https://www.kaushik.net/avinash/
35	To err is human - https://en.wiktionary.org/wiki/errare_humanum_est#Latin
36	Maslow's hierarchy of needs - https://en.wikipedia.org/wiki/Maslow's_hierarchy_of_needs
37	Unit Economics: What is a Contribution Margin? - Outlier .... https://outlier.ai/data-driven-daily/unit-economics-contribution-margin/
38	Every Unit Counts: Assessing Profitability	by Outlier AI https://outlierai.medium.com/every-unit-counts-assessing-profitability-90e0548dcc3e
39	Unit Economics: Examples of Unit Economics - Outlier AI, Inc.. https://outlier.ai/data-driven-daily/unit-economics-examples-of-unit-economics/
40	https://www.youtube.com/watch?v=7MxlVMzRxa8
41	Break-Even Point
42	https://outlier.ai/data-driven-daily/money-metrics-breaking-even/
43	Cost Of Goods Sols - https://www.investopedia.com/terms/c/cogs.asp
44	http://christophjanz.blogspot.com/2014/10/five-ways-to-build-100-million-business.html
45	Software As A Service
46	https://www.investopedia.com/terms/b/burnrate.asp
47	https://www.brex.com/blog/startup-runway/
48	https://en.wikipedia.org/wiki/Diffusion_of_innovations
49	https://www.ycombinator.com/library

50 https://www.youtube.com/watch?v=aIAbNeqn9K8
51 How to Pitch a Brilliant Idea - Harvard Business Review. https://hbr.org/2003/09/how-to-pitch-a-brilliant-idea
52 https://hbr.org/2003/09/how-to-pitch-a-brilliant-idea
53 Elevator pitch - Wikipedia. https://en.wikipedia.org/wiki/Elevator_pitch
54 KISS principle - https://en.wikipedia.org/wiki/KISS_principle
55 https://www.docsend.com/
56 https://docsend.com/view/p8jxsqr
57 Lessons From A Study of Perfect Pitch Decks: VCs Spend An https://techcrunch.com/2015/06/08/lessons-from-a-study-of-perfect-pitch-decks-vcs-spend-an-average-of-3-minutes-44-seconds-on-them/
58 A Guide to YC Demo Day Presentations: Fundraising, Pitch https://www.ycombinator.com/library/49-a-guide-to-yc-demo-day-presentations
59 https://www.ycombinator.com/library/49-a-guide-to-yc-demo-day-presentations
60 https://slidebean.com/
61 https://in.linkedin.com/in/kvaitheeswaran
62 https://www.linkedin.com/in/iyersrikanth
63 https://www.linkedin.com/in/ganeshbalakrishnan
64 https://www.linkedin.com/in/vaibhavtewari
65 Start-up Survival Links - http://bit.ly/StartupSurvivalLinks

Start-up Survival

ABOUT THE AUTHOR

Uday grew up in a typical Indian middle-class family in Bangalore, Karnataka. In a family of where his father was the first in their entire family, over many generations, to leave a salaried job and venture out on his own. He was not taught the standard script to build one's career: "work hard at school and score high" because his parents knew he was a free spirit. He graduated his 10th from Bishop Cotton's Boys School, then went on to do his PUC at Christ University (Christ College as it was known when he graduated). There was nobody to guide him about the various avenues that one may take, other than the usual Engineer, Doctor, or Architect. So the path he took was the college he was admitted to without any capitation fee. While he got his Bachelors in Chemical Engineering, dual Masters in Mechanical Engineering and Computer Science. He started his career in Europe. His first job was in the Czech Republic. Where he worked with companies like Unicorn, Infosys and DHL. Then he moved to Amsterdam, where he worked with ABN-AMRO. After which, he returned to India after having lived abroad for over a decade. In India, he joined his father's company, where he learnt a lot about managing people, growth, change management, and finance. While working with his father, he saw the opportunity to start a finishing school to fill a gap that existed between the education graduates had received and the requirement companies have. The business generated good cash but failed to scale. So he put that on the backburner and started another company that deals with quality in construction. Which grew over 300% y-o-y for 4 years before Covid struck. He is also working with his wife and 2 other friends that provides pricing of products to maximise revenue or optimal profits for e-commerce companies using AI. His ventures have been incubated at IIM-B.

www.ingramcontent.com/pod-product-compliance
Lightning Source LLC
Chambersburg PA
CBHW031535210526
45464CB00003B/1018